YOUR KNOWLEDGE HAS VALUE

Bibliographic information published by the German National Library:

The German National Library lists this publication in the National Bibliography; detailed bibliographic data are available on the Internet at http://dnb.dnb.de .

Imprint:

Copyright © 2009 GRIN Verlag, Open Publishing GmbH
Print and binding: Books on Demand GmbH, Norderstedt Germany
ISBN: 9783640461172

This book at GRIN:

http://www.grin.com/en/e-book/137523/effects-of-deregulation-in-the-aviation-industry

Barbara Bilyk

Effects of Deregulation in the Aviation Industry

GRIN Publishing

GRIN - Your knowledge has value

Since its foundation in 1998, GRIN has specialized in publishing academic texts by students, college teachers and other academics as e-book and printed book. The website www.grin.com is an ideal platform for presenting term papers, final papers, scientific essays, dissertations and specialist books.

Visit us on the internet:

http://www.grin.com/

http://www.facebook.com/grincom

http://www.twitter.com/grin_com

Effects of Deregulation in the Aviation Industry

Student name: Barbara Bilyk

Semester: Two, 2009

Introduction

Starting in the USA where deregulation of air transportation began in the late seventies, this trend was observable throughout Europe in the eighties and Australia at the beginning of the nineties. The major arguments for liberalisation were in general a reduction of capacity constraints and a simplified market access (Himpel & Lipp 2006, p.26). Constitutional for these ideas is the theory of contestable markets which assumes the efficiency of competition with a free market entry and market exit. Therefore deregulation processes aim at providing a better, safer and more efficient industry. However, Geoffrey Thomas (2008) among others points out that in reality the liberalisation of air transportation has caused predominantly negative outcomes which is why there should be a return to some degree of regulation. Based on Thomas' train of thoughts, this research paper is aimed at critically evaluating the effects of liberalisation both on the aviation industry and on the consumer. The paper is therefore structured as follows: after revealing the limitations of the evaluation, positive effects of liberalisation in Europe, the United States and Australia are outlined which are then opposed to negative effects. Based on these findings, a conclusion is finally drawn.

Evaluation

When evaluating the effects of liberalisation of air transporation, especially with regard to welfare effects, one have to keep in mind a constitutional methodological problem: at the national level, the regulated and deregulated environment never existed contemporaneously (Morrison & Winston 1986, p. 11). Another difficulty in measuring the effects is to isolate the extent to which changes are primarily imputable to liberalisation in contrast to other factors, such as technological progress (GAO 2006). That is why comparing the effects of regulation and deregulation on the industry and on the consumer is not easy to accomplish and is build on several assumptions, also called 'counterfactual construction' (Morrison & Winston 1986, p. 11).

After liberalisation of air transportation several positive outcomes occurred. One new freedom for airlines has been the ability to structure their networks independently and acquire new routes. In the intra-EU market new entrants especially low-cost carriers made use of this new possibility and started to serve routes between secondary

1

airports or even between secondary airports and foreign hubs. As a consequence, connecting passengers have a greater choice between the increased number of alternative transfer points (Gillen et al. 2001, p. 37). Like in Germany's example which can exemplify the European market, flight frequencies between these secondary airports and international hubs have increased as another consequence (Boss et al. 1996). At the same time competition between networks and between airports has increased as well. Moreover, deregulation in the EU countries has lead to lower costs and prices particularly for discount tickets. Also former flag carriers improved their productivity due to deregeulation. (Gillen et al. 2001). Finally, accident and fatality rates decreased after deregulation (Knorr 1997).

The effects listed below also support the positive outcomes of deregulation for the USA. The simplified market access allows new entrants to enter the market which is why the number of active airlines has almost doubled (Knorr 1998). This, in turn, increases competition which leads to higher productivity through higher industry capacity utilization and lower costs as well as a more efficient route network. Airlines revenues have been rising due to the increased efficiency (Hanlon 2007, p. 74). The U.S. Government Accountability Office (2006) reported that industry employment, compensation and efficiency have grown significantly after deregulation. Moreover, the average airfares dropped by nearly 40 percent in real terms since 1980. But not all routes stand to benefit in equal measures from deregulation. On congested routes airfares declined proportionally stronger than on feeder lines like for example shorter-distance and less-traveled routes. At the same time, the service measured by industry connectivity and degree of competition has been slightly improved. In general the average number of competitors increased from 2,2 per market in 1980 to 3,5 per market in 2005. Furthermore, the new opportunity for airlines to structure their route networks independently after deregulation severly accelerated the development and the use of hub-and-spoke routes (Morrison & Winston 1986, p. 5). Operating this system, airlines are able to vary the size of the planes according to the passenger volume as well as to consolidate passengers at hubs which is a reason for increased load factors. Airlines therefore stand to benefit from realising economies of scope which result in cost savings and fare reductions. At the same time, connecting passengers profit by the single-carrier service which can be offered through the hub-and-spoke network. It has been evidenced that consumers prefer this type of connection rather than having to change airlines on their journey (Carlton et al.

2

1980). This applies especially to business travellers who fly to different destinations in high frequencies (Meyers & Menzies 1999). Besides, the consumer benefits of cheaper standard ticket prices as well as a wider offer of discount tickets (Gillen et al. 2001). This is particularly true for business travellers because before liberalisation discount fares were often aligned to certain restrictions which made it impractically for business travelers to buy them (Morrison & Winston 1986). Morrison and Winston (1986; 1995) conducted an analysis to estimate the welfare effects of deregulation and found that the benefits for consumers are at an annual rate of US$ 18.4 billion.

Unlike the development in the USA after deregulation, the major route structures within Australia have not changed extremly (BTE 1993). The reasons for that are that Australia in contrast to the USA did not have a proscriptive regulation before and that Australia's air passenger market is naturally concentrated. Like in Europe and USA, Australian airfares dropped significantly after deregulation. In 1991 for instance tickets were about 21 per cent cheaper than before (BTE 1993). This development primarily affected passengers who travel on discount fares because full economy fares as well as first and business class fares increased slightly. Furthermore, there has been a strong increase in propensity to travel by air with regard to domestic flights as well as to international flights. Another outcome of deregulation in Australia is that many aspects of service quality like for instance flight frequencies have been improved or at least remained constant. Furthermore, there has been a strong growth in the airline outputs. According to the report revealed by the Australian Bureau of Transport and Communications Economics (1993), the total net gains in economic welfare after deregulation in Australia is about AUD$ 100 Million per year and the distinct winner of deregulation is the consumer.

In contrast to these arguments confirming the eligibility of deregulation, there are also some negative effects which have to be considered. Although market concentration decreased in the years right after the deregulation in the United States that might have only been a short-term effect since concentration rose again in the eighties and nineties. This is mainly due to the strong competitive forces which pushed several airlines into bankruptcy or mergers (Hanlon 2007, p. 75). Especially airlines that predated liberalisation, called legacy airlines, suffer from an increased precariousness in their financial health. United and US Airways for instance have gone bankrupt and had to terminate their pension plans for which the Pension Benefit

Guaranty Corporation had to pay almost US$ 10 billion (GAO 2006). But it is difficult to isolate the impact of deregulation at that point since broad economic factors, poor management decisions and inadequate pension regulation have to be considered at the same time. Likewise, certain hub airports are also dominated by only a few airlines which, in turn, leads to higher ticket prices than on other routes (Borenstein 1992). According to Dempsey (2008) these financial losses do not outweigh the savings on the consumer side. Besides, industry profitability and the return on investment have become much more cyclical and volatile (GAO 2006; Dempsey 2008). In order to counteract this fierce competition, incumbents have been making use of aggressive pricing and scheduling (Hanlon 2007). The power of incumbents is even reinforced through the following effects: entry barriers are created through certain marketing activities like for instance frequent flyer programs as well as scarcitiy of slots and gates enable incumbents to exert their power and exclude potential new entrants (Gillen et al 2001). According to Dempsey (2008) the reason for that development is that 'financially corrosive aspects of airline regulation were left in place'.

In Australia airline revenues dropped about twenty per cent after deregulation and like in Quantas example financial performance has been fairly uneven since then. An important constraint on airline perfomance in Australia has been high dept burdens. Comparing these outcomes to positive effects of deregulation in Australia, the BTE report (1993) declares the airlines as loosers of the reforms.

Taking all the different effects of deregulation into account, it is obvious that the air transportation industry has been going through some servere difficulties after deregulation. The transition also has been much more time-consuming than expected before and has still not reached a long-run equilibrium (Morrison & Winston 1995, p. 162). Nevertheless, liberalisation has benefited the public interest way more effectively than regulation would have (Morrison & Winston 1986, p. 72). Airlines and most passengers have been served by deregulation and the further evolution of the air transportation industry might even advance these postive otucomes (Morrison & Winston 1995, p. 162). According to Morrison & Winston (1995) there is 'no evidence that justifies regulations, new regulations, or a more activist antitrust policy'. In the same way, the US Government Accountability Office (2006) draws the conclusion that a return to regulate the industry is likely to 'reverse much of the benefits that consumers have gained and would not save airline pensions'. According to that report, the only reason for re-regulation is inadequate competition which cannot in general be said about the US air transportation industry. Restraining the forces that account for the occured dislocations would reverse the gains that have emerged at the same time, especially with regard to lower airfares. Hence, the GAO (2006) suggests direct subsidies like for example the Essentail Air Service program as a solution. Likewise Williams (2002) argues that sustainable competitive conditions that have been produced by free market forces should not be affected by new regulatory intervention since that would interefere the positive effects. But he also outlines that there are certain circumstances in which regulation is highly beneficial to the consumer. Williams (2002) therefore suggests to move 'the regulatory pendulum back a little from its totally free market stop point'. For this reason, he also differentiates between two dimensions of regulation: consisten international rules and national regulatory frameworks. Both should be aimed at assuring progressive competition and not interfere innovation. Similarily, Gillen et al. (2001) conclude that there is a need for deregulation to be accompanied by 'effective competition policy measures' (Gillen et al 2001, p. 44). The reason for that is that competition in the air transportation industry is practicable but not perfect. Therefore, no regulatory control mechanisms like before liberalisation are needed but in order to assure the durability of positive effects competition policy tools such as bilateral air service agreements should be applied.

Conclusion

At present, the market organisation of the air transportation industry is in principle charactarised by a tendency towards liberalisation of the relevant framework requirement for airlines. The resulting effects of deregulation are diverse but similar in the countries under consideration. The consumer benefits all in all from increased flight frequencies, a denser network, lower airfares as well as an increased service. Howerver, the effects on the air transportation industry are not as distinct as for the consumer. Although productivity and revenues have increased, there have been also severe issues concerning the financial health of airlines as well as bankruptcies and mergers. Concluding from these outcomes, one could say that the winners of deregulation are the consumers whereas the airlines are the loosers (BTE 1993). When relating these findings to Geoffrey Thomas' (2008) article, there is evidence for his thesis concerning the return to regulation. However, re-regulation should not be as far-ranging as the regulative framework before since that would diminish the positive effects of competition. The regulative institutions should instead focus on making use of tools that benefit the consumer and the industry at the same time without interfering positive market forces.

Bibliography

Australian Bureau of Transport and Communications Economics (BTE) 1993, *The progress of aviation reform*. Report No. 81, June 1993.

Borenstein, S. 1992, *The Evolution of U.S. airline competition*. Journal of Economic Perspectives Vol. 6, p. 45 – 73.

Boss, E.J. et al 1996, *Deregulierung in Deutschland. Eine empirische Analyse (Deregulation in Germany. An empirical analysis)*. Kieler Studien. Tübingen.

Carlton, D.W.; Landes, W.M; Posner, R.A. 1980, *Benefits and Costs of Airline Mergers: A case study*. Bell Journal of Economics Vol. 11 (Spring 1980), p. 65 – 83.

Dempsey, P.S. 2008, *The financial performance of the airline industry post-deregulation*. Houston Law Review Vol. 45 No. 2 (Summer 2008).

Gillen, D.W. et al 2001, *The impact of liberalizing international aviation bilaterals*. Ashgate Aldershot.

Hanlon, P. 2007, *Global airlines. Competition in a transnational industry*. 3rd Edition, Elsevier.

Himpel, F. & Lipp, R. 2006, *Luftverkehrsallianzen (air transportation alliances)*. Wiesbaden.

Knorr, A. 1997, *Wettbewerb und Flugsicherheit – ein Widerspruch? Eine ökonomische Analyse am Beispiel des amerikanischen Luftverkehrsmarktes (Competition and flight safety – a contradiction? An economic analysis on the US-American air transportation market)*. Zeitschrift für Verkehrswissenschaft Vol. 68, p. 94 – 122.

Knorr, A. 1998, *Zwanzig Jahre Deregulierung im US-Luftverkehr – eine Zwischenbilanz (Twenty years of deregulation in US air transportation – an interim result).* ORDO Jahrbuch für die Ordnung in Wirtschaft und Gesellschaft Vol. 49, p. 419 – 464.

Morrison, S. & Winston, C. 1986, *The economic effects of airlilne deregulation.*Washington DC: The Brookings Institution.
Morrison, S. & Winston, C. 1995, *The evolution of Airline Industry*, Washington DC: The Brookings Institution.

Myers, J.R. & Menzies, T.R. 1999, *Airline deregulation – Time to complete the job.* Issues in Science and Technology Vol. 16 Iss. 2 (December 1999), p. 24 – 29.

Thomas, G. 2008, *Deregulation takes heavy toll.* The Australian, 10.03.2008.

U.S. Government Accountability Office (GAO) 2006, *Airline Deregulation-Reregulating the Airline Industry would likely reverse consumer benefits and not save airline pensions.* Report to Congressional Committees GAO-06-630.

Williams, G. 2002, *Airline competition: Deregulation's Mixed Legacy.* Ashgate: Aldershot.

YOUR KNOWLEDGE HAS VALUE

- We will publish your bachelor's and
  master's thesis, essays and papers

- Your own eBook and book -
  sold worldwide in all relevant shops

- Earn money with each sale

Upload your text at www.GRIN.com
and publish for free